The Failure of Britain's Police

The Failure of Britain's Police:
London and New York Compared

Norman Dennis
George Erdos
David Robinson

with an Introduction by
George L. Kelling

Author of
*Fixing Broken Windows: Restoring Order
and Reducing Crime in Our Communities*

Civitas: Institute for the Study of Civil Society
London

First published April 2003
Civitas
The Mezzanine, Elizabeth House
39 York Road, London SE1 7NQ
email: books@civitas.org.uk

ISBN 1-903 386-26-8

Typeset by Civitas
in New Century Schoolbook

Printed in Great Britain by
The Cromwell Press
Trowbridge, Wiltshire

Contents

Authors

Norman Dennis was Reader in Social Studies at the University of Newcastle upon Tyne, and is now a Visiting Fellow there. He is Director of Community Studies at Civitas. He spent 2002 studying trends in crime and the police responses to it, with the resources and within the culture in which they had to operate, in London, New York and Paris, with study visits to Chicago and St Louis. A full account of his research on changes in crime, culture and policing in London, New York, Paris and Berlin is in preparation. He has been active in the Labour Party since 1946.

George Erdos is senior lecturer in the School of Biology (Psychology) at the University of Newcastle upon Tyne, and a chartered occupational psychologist. He is currently studying those arrangements in personal relationships, organisations and societies that have been relatively successful in producing personal freedom, mutual trust, willing co-operation and an adequate and secure standard of living for all participants—the traditional concerns of English ethical socialism. Dr Erdos is intimately acquainted with the repressive systems of both national-socialist Germany and communist Hungary. He argues, therefore, with his fellow authors, that in societies enjoying historically high levels of freedom of expression, and governments that cannot use much fraud or any force to prevent the electorate legally removing them from office, the greatest threat to freedom originates with the law-breaker in the state and the rule-breaker in the voluntary organisation.

David Robinson is a graduate of the University of Newcastle upon Tyne. He has been active in Labour causes in South Tyneside for many years, and has been a volunteer worker in several public-service organisations. He is currently an officer in the Co-operative movement. He is an adult education teacher, specialising in local working-class history.

Acknowledgement

We are grateful to Reform for support towards the cost of this project.

Introduction

George L. Kelling

National stereotypes are usually several generations out of date. We Americans are still inclined
to see England as a haven of civil tranquility in a
crime-ridden world. One American recalls, perhaps,
Sherlock Holmes in the *Study in Scarlet*, where he
complains about the inevitable boredom of a detec-
tive's job in London, because in London there is no
crime. Another perhaps has seen a rerun on afternoon
television of Ronald Coleman as Bulldog Drummond,
where he refuses to take seriously the case of a girl
who appeals for his help because her parents have
been abducted in leafy Godalming. He grandly dis-
misses her story as absurd. 'My dear, you are an
American. Such things don't happen in England.'

The social critic George Orwell wrote in 1944 of the
striking impression made on foreigners by the 'orderly
behaviour of English crowds, the lack of pushing and
quarrelling' and by the fact that except for 'certain
well-defined areas' in only half-a-dozen big towns,
there was 'very little crime or violence'. It was the view
of the historian K.B. Smellie, unsuspecting of what
was about to befall, that the life of English towns had
steadily improved. 'The contemporary English', he
wrote in the 1950s, 'have as unaggressive a public life
as any recorded people.' In civilian life, the anthropolo-
gist Geoffrey Gorer wrote, 'the English are certainly
among the most peaceful, gentle, courteous and
orderly populations that the civilised world has ever

1

seen'. He added, 'You hardly ever see a fight in a bar (a not uncommon sight in most of the rest of Europe or the USA), and football crowds are as orderly as church meetings'.

An American scholar is likely to feel that his stereotype of crime-free England is confirmed when he sees that the official crime statistics do not deal at all with offences involving weapons until the 1970s. The first time that English police officers were equipped with as much as a plastic riot shield was in 1977, when they were issued as protection in the expectation of a clash between members of the National Front and of the Socialist Workers' Party.

England was widely perceived in the world, not only in America, as an orderly society of law and justice, lightly controlled because control was willingly accepted. It was the English, by the way, who enlightened Americans about how to police a democracy. Although American police forgot his lessons during the 1960s and 1970s, Sir Robert Peel taught Americans that peace could be kept by peaceful means, that the true measure of police was the absence of crime, that police could be mere citizens—not military troops—who are paid to do what is everyone's responsibility, and that crime can be prevented by police presence and persuasion and by maintaining order and reducing opportunities for crime.

The American's stereotype of England that crystallized out of his own experience, travelers' tales, or the reality indicated by statistics and the contemporary social comment of both foreign and domestic scholars, disintegrated only gradually in the face of rapidly rising crime rates from the middle of the 1950s. Crimes recorded by the English police peaked in 1992, but the number and rate remained very high as compared with the period before 1955.

What is of particular fascination to an American observer of crime and, practically, its control by different national and local police forces, is the astonishing rise in England in the number of street crimes. This rise did not abate in 1992 with the total crime figure. It continued strongly until special measures to combat the rise were introduced ten years later.

Attitudes to crime and the role of the police, including the readiness to accept or dismiss whole bodies of statistical data, have been and are colored by politics in both our countries. Nowadays, our 'liberals' and your 'left' tend to be critical of the police and sympathetic to the criminal, who is seen as the product of unjust social conditions and even as an admirable rebel against them. They find as their strange bedfellows new elements of 'the right'. The 'freedom of the individual' to lead his or her own life socially and personally, and not just in entering into voluntary economic contracts, is for them the highest of all values. Older elements of 'the right' demand the restoration of 'law and order', if necessary by harsh and repressive measures.

Our liberals and your left point to corporate frauds, any one of which involves the misappropriation of sums that exceed all the robberies that take place in a year, and damage to the environment before which vandalism pales into insignificance. But the effects of white-collar crime are in the typical case dissipated and remote. The immediacy of street crime and of local nuisances make them in the normal case *felt* as a much larger factor, in the areas where they occur, than even the most heinous white-collar crimes in determining the quality of everyday life. The contribution that the police can make to the reduction of street crime is therefore a matter of urgent public policy, especially for the protection of people in some of the poorest areas or our cities.

A valuable feature of this book is that all the authors are of the Left—two of them are long-standing members of, by American standards, left-wing parties. What they have to say cannot be dismissed easily, therefore, as the opinion of hard-line Republicans, or in English terms, as the voice of 'the forces of conservatism'.

Street crime in New York City, and the more effective and less effective responses of the NYPD, have for many years been topics at the center of the research and policy concerns of the School of Criminal Justice's Police Institute at Rutgers University, Newark, whose northern horizon is dominated by the towers of Manhattan. Civitas is to be congratulated in producing a fresh and vivacious account, well grounded in the data, of New York's recent policing experiences, and of what London might be able to learn—or rather, as the authors suggest, relearn—from those experiences.

George L. Kelling, Faculty Chair
Police Institute, School of Criminal Justice
Rutgers University

The Failure of Britain's Police:
London and New York Compared

Recent trends in street crime and its control in London and New York present a striking contrast. London was for long a by-word in the world for law-abidingness and the effective policing of its safe streets. New York was a by-word for the severity of its street crime, especially in the 1970s and the 1980s. In the 1990s their situations were sharply reversed. In 1991 there were 22,000 robberies in London.[1] In 2002 there were 44,600, an increase of 105 per cent.[2] In 1991 there were 99,000 robberies in New York City. In 2002 there were 27,000, a decrease of 73 per cent.[3] To draw equal with New York's achievement, London would thus have to gain no fewer than 178 percentage points in its fight against street crime. Since 1994 New York has adopted the policy of greatly increasing the numbers of police officers, and confidently attacking trivial crime and disorder, regarding them as the seedbed of worse things. London, as in the 'Lambeth experiment' (see p. 16), has opted to concentrate its much smaller numbers on serious crimes. Nationally, we have chosen to throw in the sponge because the forces of law and order, whether formal or informal, have lost control of the situation, and spuriously justify the legalisation or decriminalisation of many offences on the grounds that none of them are so bad after all.

New York's annual robbery rate is now less than 540 per 100,000 population. London's is 620.

Street Crime and Policing in London

The change in the policing of street crime in London has partly taken the form of urgent measures. In

7

February 2002, 'Operation Safer Streets' put 5,000 extra officers into the nine London boroughs regarded as street-crime hot spots. In March, London was included in a national Street-Crime Initiative that carried special funding of £65 million for the ten police force areas that the scheme eventually covered. At a cost estimated to be £14,500 for each mugging prevented,[4] the surging crime on London's streets that had taken place in 2001 was cut back—but only to a number that was still approximately a tenth higher than it had been even in the previous muggings-plagued year of 2000. The Home Office's press release said that the new figures showed that the 'escalating trend' in street crime was now 'under control' and 'going down'.[5] In December 2000 there had been 1,038 snatch thefts and 3,008 robberies of personal property in London—making a total of 4,046 muggings. In December 2002 there were 1,548 snatch thefts and 2,880 robberies of personal property—making a total of 4,428 muggings, an increase of nine per cent.[6]

The Metropolitan police are to be congratulated in bringing street crime from the level of 2001 to a level nevertheless still above that of 2000. But financial resources on the scale of £14,000 or £15,000 per mugging saved are not likely to be endlessly committed by any government. The diversion of large teams of officers from other duties is necessarily a temporary expedient, and the meagre results are not likely to be approved in the long run by any electorate. By contrast, New York's police actually did adopt (as distinct from claiming it had adopted) not only a more effective, but also a more sustainable strategy—simply employing more police officers, and seeing that they were neither in police stations nor in automobiles, but patrolling their beats on foot, conspicuously looking after the interests of the law-abiding and reasonably considerate and tolerant citizen. According to the Home Office's own research, 77 per cent of the population in Britain has some confidence that the criminal justice system protects the rights of people accused of crimes. But only 32 per cent now has any confidence that it protects the rights of the victims. (Within the criminal justice system, the courts and the 'penal' system are probably much more the objects of blame than the police.)[7]

The rise in crime generally since 1955

Crime rose rapidly in this country after 1955. That essential point, the explosion of crime from 1955-92 and the continuing historically very high level, is sometimes overlooked when 'the rise in crime' is taken to have started with Thatcherism. It is assumed that, as far as law-abidingness is concerned, the country would be somehow back to normal if it could return to the figures of the early 1980s.

The police did indeed record 'only' 2.5 million crimes in England and Wales in 1980, and recorded a rise of two million crimes by 1998/99, to 4.5 million. But the starting point of 2.5 million crimes in the pre-Thatcher years was itself an astonishingly high figure by the standards of previous generations. The difficulty is not to find the numbers but for them to be believed, so incredibly small do they seem to a later generation.

In 1955, fewer than 0.5 million crimes were recorded. In 1960, 0.8 million. In 1970, 1.6 million. In 1980, 2.5 million. In 1990, 4.4 million. The figure peaked in 1992, when 5.1 million crimes were recorded.[8] The series is broken in 1992, when figures on a new basis included more offences as 'crimes'. On the new basis the crime figures show a 22 per cent fall from 5.6 million in 1992 to 4.5 million in 1998/99. The series was again broken in 1998/99. The figures on the new basis of comparability show a rise from 5.1 million in 1998/99 to 5.3 million in 1999/2000, and a fall from 5.3 million in 1999/2000 to 5.2 million in 2000/01.[9]

The best estimate for the latest period is that, when the difficulties of comparability are laboriously calculated, there has been another 'real' increase of about two per cent in all crimes recorded by the police in 2001/02 as compared with 2000/01.[10]

These falls in the overall crime rate since 1992, and a rise of 'only' two per cent last year, have been spun—and naively accepted—as a reason for congratulations all round.[11]

In January 2003 a Home Office publication asserted that the chance of being a crime victim *'remains historically low'*.[12] In 1972 there was a total of 1.7 million crimes.[13] In 2002 there were 5.8 million crimes.[14] In 1972 firearms were used in the commission of 2,100 crimes; in 2001/02 firearms were used in the commission of 22,300 crimes. In 1972 handguns were used 254 times; in 2001/02, 5,900 times. In 1972 firearms were used in 570 robberies; in 2001/02 in 5,500 robberies. 1,970 of these 5,500 armed robberies were armed robberies on the public highway. In 1972 there were 8,900 robberies *in the whole of England and Wales*; in 2001/02 there were almost as many, 6,500, *in the London borough of Lambeth alone*.[15]

Our problem, then, is only partly the rise in the crime rate since the Thatcher years, ameliorated by some remission in the 1990s. It is the fundamental shift within two or three generations, and especially the enormous shift that began about 1955, in the law-abidingness and 'policeability' of the English.

The causes of the fall in crime in the 1990s

The fall in the numbers of crimes recorded by the police *other than street crime* from 1992 to 2002 was mainly associated with improved security measures of a physical and commercial or personal kind, rather than with either 'better behaviour' or more effective policing. Cars have electronic immobilisers and better locks. That is one of the reasons why cars are now stolen while the owner is in the car, when the security provided by the manufacturer is in abeyance and the motorist's only protection is a law-abiding population and an effective police presence. Blocks of flats have entry phones and cameras. The windows and doors of dwellings are dead-bolted. People are more careful with their belongings. They avoid known trouble spots. They remain longer within the safety of their homes.

As Dr. Paul McGrail of the Open University showed at the 1999 conference of the Royal Geographical Society, electronic surveillance is effective in blocks of flats, where the residents themselves are constant monitors.[16] But CCTV images from street cameras are much less likely to be monitored than CCTV images in blocks of flats and shops. Camera surveillance is effective when the photographs can easily identify the culprit long after the offence—speed cameras show the licence plate of the vehicle—or when quick action can be taken by the co-ordination of camera surveillance and police intervention, as in Oxford Street. When the CCTV picture does not activate a quick response; or where the culprit can conceal his or her identity; or where the culprit, even if the image is clear, is difficult to trace, then the deterrent effect can be weak. A Home Office study revealed in 2002 a very mixed picture of the effects of camera surveillance on street crime.[17]

The continuing rise in street crime throughout the 1990s

Ordinarily, then, the control of crime *on the streets* is out of the hands of the individual citizen. On the street, even the wife of a recent Home Secretary—the Minister responsible for the Metropolitan Police—could find herself the victim of a robbery in Pimlico and, a few weeks before, the son of the Prime Minister was mugged.[18] Street safety, where it is not the product of civic virtue, is essentially in the hands of the police. In a few cases it is in the hands of commerce (the immobilisation of stolen mobile phones can be expected to have a strong impact on mobile-phone robberies). And *on the streets* the crime rate did not fall in the 1990s.

The easiest index of the rise and fall of what is implied by the vague term 'street crime' is the figure for all robberies.[19] Statistics for robberies of personal property are not always available. It is fairly easy to add snatch thefts. Doing so produces the same trend as robbery itself.

When the effects of the new rules for counting crimes are taken into consideration, the recorded steep rise in the number of cases of 'violence against the person' is shown to have been actually a *decline* of five per cent. But robbery—theft or attempted theft with violence or the threat of violence—is one of the crime categories that has *not* been significantly affected by the new counting rules. We can still tell what has been happening *here*, and ignore the usual bamboozlement of those commentators who necessarily do not have any other figures of their own, but who dismiss as useless all crime figures that do not support their prejudices or political wishes. Rises and falls in the *robbery* figures, unlike other official figures, have *not* been rendered difficult to disentangle by transitional changes in counting methods.[20]

The number of robberies of personal and business property in England and Wales, hardly touched by recording difficulties, continued its rise throughout the 1990s (with some annual fluctuations) and the rise *accelerated* between 2000/01 and 2001/02. Robberies in England and Wales rose from 53,000 in 1992 to over 95,000 in 2000/01, and then jumped in a single year to an astounding 121,000 in 2001/02 (see Figure 1, p. 14). Recorded robberies of personal property alone rose from 83,000 in 2000/01 to 108,000 in 2001/02.[21]

The Metropolitan Police did not aim to reduce street crime. It gave itself the target only of keeping street crime at its existing level. Its performance fell short of the target in 1999/2000, when street crime rose by 36 per cent. Its performance fell short of target again in 2000/01, when street crime rose by a further 18 per cent above the 2000/01 figure. The annual report that provides this information says: 'London is now a safer place to work and live in'.[22]

In April 2001 there were 443 robberies of personal property in the borough of Lambeth. This rose to 620 robberies in September 2001, an increase of 177 (there were also 242 snatches of personal property during the month). This increase in robberies of personal property in one London borough in half a year was more than the total for all robberies for the whole of England and Wales in eight of the ten years 1920 to 1929.[23] By December 2002, the number of robberies of personal property in Lambeth was down to 282 in the month. Again, this figure for one month in one London borough was in excess of that for all robberies, personal and business, for the whole of England and Wales in the whole of any year between the two world

14

Figure 1
Robberies recorded by the police, England and Wales, 1970 to 2002

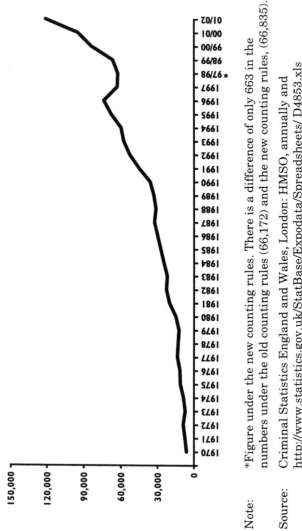

Note: *Figure under the new counting rules. There is a difference of only 663 in the numbers under the old counting rules (66,172) and the new counting rules, (66,835).

Source: Criminal Statistics England and Wales, London: HMSO, annually and http://www.statistics.gov.uk/StatBase/Expodata/Spreadsheets/D4853.xls

15

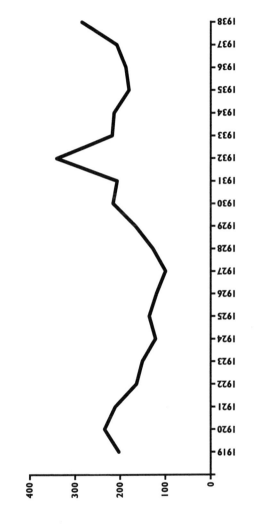

Figure 2
Robberies recorded by the police, England and Wales, 1919 to 1938

Source: *Criminal Statistics, England and Wales*, London: HMSO, annually and
http://www.statistics.gov.uk/StatBase/Expodata/Spreadsheets/D4853.xls

wars except in the depths of the Depression, in 1932, and just before the Second World War, in 1938 (see Figure 2, p. 15).

In a special analysis of police files on 2,000 cases of the robbery of personal property in the spring and summer of 2001, Home Office research staff found that there had been a 'marked increase' in the 1990s in the number of younger victims and offenders. The number of 11-to-15-year-olds charged with robbery increased five-fold between 1992 and 2001. In 2001, 22 per cent of robberies involved children as victims, and just over half of the perpetrators were aged between 16 and 20. Regardless of the age of the victim or offender, 35 per cent of robberies were of a mobile phone.[24]

Targeting serious crimes

Police efforts also took the form of leaving 'trivial' crime and disorder to take care of itself, to allow the police to concentrate on serious crimes and important perpetrators. This strategy gained wide notice due to an accident of publicity surrounding the policy when it was first introduced. The policy of ignoring minor, and concentrating on major crimes had been given prominence by the commander of London's Lambeth police area, especially in his announcement that the public consumption of cannabis would, from now on, be the subject only of confiscation and a police warning. In the early stages of his policy's implementation, the commander was accused by his male lover of smoking cannabis with him in the flat they shared. The commander denied that he himself had smoked cannabis. There were other allegations levelled against him. The policy and its background were fully dealt with by Commander Paddick in the popular press.[25] Ignoring 'trivial' and 'victimless' crimes was exactly the opposite of the policy implemented by the New York Police Department under Mayor Giuliani in the 1990s.

Much lip service is undoubtedly paid to the importance of 'the bobby on the beat'. In one town where bicycle police patrols have been introduced, and the existence and increased numbers of police officers as 'beat managers' have been publicised, the Chief Inspector in charge nevertheless warned people in the areas concerned that because his officers were not in police cars, a response to a call about, for example, noisy youths would take ... several days. In another police area, the sides of the local buses advertise that the police force has responded to the wishes of the public by carrying out a reorganisation that puts police officers on foot in the community. In the town centre shopping precincts pairs of foot-patrol officers can now be seen more often than previously, but rarely elsewhere.

'Multi-agency', 'problem-solving' and other 'partnerships' using titles borrowed from New York abound. In New York these terms mean bringing other resources to bear directly on the solution of the immediate problem of crime, disorder or nuisance. But sharing responsibility with local government employees and elected representatives, with health service workers and probation officers, to solve the deeper problems in the long term, and so forth, can easily prove a mechanism for one set of people with useless or harmful policies, or no policies at all, passing the buck around to other sets of people with equally inefficacious or harmful policies.

The police overwhelmed by crime

Official publications show the ratio of the total population to the number of police officers. On that measure, governments can boast of an increase in police establishments and in the numbers of officers employed. They do not show a far more important figure, that of the ratio of crimes to the number of police officers. On that measure, crime has overwhelmed police forces.

Whatever the arguments about the reliability of crime statistics for any other purposes, they are not relevant here. The number crimes that eventually appear in the official statistics, for whatever reason, is the number that the police have had to deal with in some way.

In 1955 in New York there were 22,600 police officers. There were 7,400 reported robberies. There were therefore 33 reported robberies to every 100 police officers.[26] By 1993 police numbers increased to 29,000. The increase in crime far outpaced this. There were 86,000 reported robberies. Even with the larger police force, then, in 1993 there were not 33, but 296 robberies to every 100 police officers.

But by 2002 New York was getting a grip on the crime/police situation. The number of police officers was up to 40,000. The number of reported robberies was down to 27,000. In 2002 there were therefore 68 reported robberies per 100 officers. This was still twice the rate of 1955, but only a quarter of the rate of 1993.[27]

London, in stark contrast, was not getting a grip on the situation. In London there had been a similar gradual expansion in police numbers since 1955, so that by 1993 London had 23,000 police officers. But there had also been, as there had been in New York, a very steep rise in the number of reported crimes the police had to deal with. In 1993 there were 24,000 robberies, extraordinarily high by past English standards. There were, therefore, 105 robberies per 100 police officers. This was still only about a third of New York's crime/police ratio.[28] In 2002 in London there were 26,000 police officers.[29] But the number of reported robberies nearly doubled, from 24,000 in 1993 to 45,000 in 2002.[30] The London ratio of 170 robberies per 100 officers was now two and a half times the New York ratio.

In spite of wishful thinking and propaganda celebrations of marginal increases in police numbers, the growth of crime made it impossible for the British police officer to be effectively and normally, as distinct from symbolically and rarely, any longer, part of a preventive crime force—to be the foot-patrolling or cycle-patrolling bobby on the beat. Most of the working time of the majority of police officers had to be spent in reacting to calls to crimes already committed, and then doing the paper work in the police station prior to processing suspects through the courts. The explosion in crime since the mid-1950s, peaking in 1992 so far as crimes of all types is concerned, but continuing to rise rapidly on the street throughout the 1990s and the first years of the 2000s, meant that without significant rises in police numbers, preventive beat policing was a pipe dream or a deliberately deceptive political promise.

The growing discrepancy over the previous 30 years between the number of reported crimes and the number of police officers is shown in Table 1 (p. 20) for the whole of England and Wales and for all crimes.[31]

When the immediate *policing* problem is not addressed, it can easily come to appear to the victim that the implicit bargain between the public and police is being violated. The original bargain was: 'I'll give up my right to self-protection. I also give up my right to prevent people behaving in such a way that a large variety of other behaviours by other people are prevented or hindered. In exchange, I shall enjoy the far more predictable, efficient and fair protection of my own person and property, and the protection of the system of the agreed rules that maximise the scope for freely chosen activities, that a specialised police force acting under public control provides. That is the major bargain. But as a corollary, that bargain being kept, I accept that this means that the police will then properly prevent me from acting on my own behalf to protect myself, and prevent me from public-spiritedly acting to protect the freedom of many people to engage in a large number of activities against people who restrict that freedom by their invasive activities.'

Table 1
Comparison between reported crimes and the number of police officers, England and Wales, 1971-2001

Year	Crimes reported (thousands)	Police officers (thousands)	Crimes per police officer (number)
1971	1,666	97	17
1981	2,794	120	23
1991	5,075	127	40
2001	5,527	126	44

It can sometimes seem that when the police do not or cannot uphold the major clause of the bargain (for whatever good reason of insufficient resources or a hostile culture), the part that they pay most attention to, because it involves the exercise of their authority over the part of the population that is most ready to accept it, is the subsidiary prohibition on self-protection.

What used to be regarded with approval as 'self-policing' when practised by a group or neighbourhood, and as 'good citizenship' when practiced by an individual, is condemned as 'vigilantism'—a term that conjures up, and is intended to conjure up, images of innocent men lynched by hate-filled mobs of violent and ignorant bigots under the flare of torches in some remote Mississippi town in the 1920s.[32]

New Yorkers can still envy Londoners' civic virtues and admire the qualities of the Metropolitan Police in many respects. London is still a wonderfully civilised city. Over a wide range of policing problems, the London police are highly effective and remain surprisingly amiable. They have special units whose expertise is unmatched elsewhere. Never a corrupt force on the scale often achieved elsewhere, since the internal reforms of Commissioner Robert Mark the Metropolitan Police service has been as free from corruption as probably any force in the world.[33] But has London anything to learn from New York about the policing of street crime?

Street Crime and Policing in New York

New York started with far worse problems of street crime than London has ever had, or is ever likely to have. But in recent years it has done a far better job in tackling its problems of street crime than London has in solving London's problems.

Although New York had never been famed as a law-abiding city, its street-crime problem sharply worsened in the mid-1970s. There was a multitude of coincident causes,[34] among them serious budgetary problems that afflicted the city from 1975 to 1983, some of them the direct result of the sharp increase in welfare costs. A famous front page headline of the New York *Daily News* announced on 30 October 1975 the decision of the President of the United States not to rescue it from its financial difficulties: 'Ford to City: Drop Dead'.[35] One of the city's solutions was to economise on its police force.

Faced with growing crime and disorder since the early 1960s, the police department had been expanding. In 1968 alone it brought in an extra 3,600 recruits, raising the number of uniformed officers to 29,900. Over 1,000 more civilians were also recruited. The particular significance of these increases was noted by the police commissioner, E.R. Leary, as greatly increasing the NYPD's 'street patrol strength'.[36] By 1974 the number of uniformed officers had slowly increased to reach 30,600.[37] Eight years of cuts followed, and the low-point of 21,800 was reached in January 1982.[38]

Quite suddenly, crime and disorder on its streets meant that New York's demise as a functioning city was routinely expected.[39] The novelist Saul Bellow remarks somewhere that 'New York makes you think about the collapse of civilisation. ... Many people already bank on it'. Jason Epstein, a leader of New York's cultural elite, and in 1970 the defender of the Chicago Seven's right to foment an intensely violent riot against (and by) the police at the Democratic National Convention in 1968, later came to write an article called 'The tragical history of New York', in which he declared that the city's engine had failed, and it was adrift on an uncharted sea.

New York was frequently portrayed in the cinema as a place of violent nihilistic shoot-outs or as a city that had turned into a junk yard or even an enormous walled-in prison ruled by under-class war-lords (*The*

Warriors [1979], *Escape from New York* [1981]). Tom Wolfe's *The Bonfire of the Vanities* (1987), depicting the chaos in the judicial system under the pressure of lawlessness on New York's streets, was made into a film as well as being a famous book. The *Death Wish* films appealed to audiences who felt that neither the police nor the courts were any longer capable of containing street crime.

The acute and chronic shortage of patrol officers made the NYPD into a reactive force. It did not have the resources to notice and process 'trivial' and 'victimless' crimes. But as often happens, a virtue was made out of necessity. It came to seem good policy to overlook petty crime and disorder, and to deal only with major crimes after they had been committed. 'Arrests' of 'real' criminals became the criterion for success, not the old Peelite criterion of a low crime rate. And, of course, a high rate of arrests was an achievement that could go on forever, if the crime rate was rising. The smaller the police force, the more repressive it became.

What happened in Times Square can be selected as a particularly vivid example of a widespread process. Before the 1970s, Times Square was a safe place. Its problems began when the NYPD ignored street prostitution and 'soft' drug use, and according to the 'broken windows' theory that will be dealt with below, *because* they ignored these trivial offences. With prostitutes on the street at all hours, some of them taking drugs to keep themselves going, the drug dealers came in. According to the economic maxim 'supply creates its own demand', users followed the dealers. The prostitutes' clients, the johns, proved easy targets for robbers and car thieves. Rubbish was discarded everywhere. The walls became the target of paint-sprayers, until nothing but graffiti, unsightly to most people, praised only by those for whom dissidence is a principle, could be seen on the walls. Fights over prostitutes and drugs led to assaults and homicides.

Places like Washington Square Park became a drugs bazaar, where Ivy League students could step out the doors of New York University to keep themselves supplied with marijuana. Bryant Park, right next to New York City's magnificent privately funded public library, became a no-go area for ordinary workers in the daytime, and for visitors to the area in the evening. Hard-drug availability and use followed 'harmless' drug availability and use.

The police, furthermore, were intimidated by the now normal reaction of the broadsheet press and mainstream news media to any *enforcement* of law and order by the police. Paradoxically, the concentration on the police of the right to enforce public order, and the high degree of public order that resulted from that, had depended upon a growing abhorrence of the use of any private violence. This abhorrence spread to the police's use of any force. The idea gained ground—a self-indulgence possible only in a society with a long history of civic safety—that if civilians doing illegal things used illegal force against the police, the justice of their grievances exonerated them, and the police were to blame if they used force to maintain or restore lawful conduct.

A clear example was the intimidation of the police in the aftermath of the Tompkins Square Park riot in August 1988, reminiscent of the intimidation of the Metropolitan Police by the Macpherson inquiry of 1998.[40] Tompkins Square Park is located in East Village, a racially, ethnically, economically and politically diverse corner of the lower east side of

Manhattan. It had been known since the 1960s for its tolerance of a wide variety of lifestyles. But by 1988 the tolerance of the residents around the park was wearing thin as one of the 'lifestyles' stifled the possibility of people pursuing many other lifestyles.

Individual residents, as well as local block associations and community boards, increasingly complained to the police about disorderly groups of men and women who were playing loud music in the park and generally partying from 9 p.m. to 5 a.m. Drugs traffickers were using the park to shield their activities from police observation. Large numbers of the intentionally homeless, as well as the unintentionally homeless and mentally ill, preferred summer residence in the park to either gainful employment or the services of the city's Human Services Administration. However carefully private or public owners of property had faced, painted or decorated the walls of their buildings to suit their own tastes within the limits of what was aesthetically acceptable to neighbours and passers-by, individual graffitists decided that every sprayable surface should bear their signature, and take on the appearance they alone dictated. Litter, used condoms, discarded needles and human waste abounded. The police accordingly moved in to enforce the park's ordinances and the 'quality of life'—the general public's quality of life—regulations of the city.

The park's closing hour was 1 a.m. Occupants of the park were required to leave at closing time, though the police made the concession of allowing homeless people to remain in one part of the park. The curfew was strongly supported by local residents and their representative organisations, but opposed over several weeks of discussions and rallies by the park's occupiers. On the night of 6-7 August, however, demonstrators threw bricks, bottles and fireworks at the police. The local police called for the assistance of officers from other precincts, and eventually not only mounted police, but a police helicopter was involved in the incident.

The police on the scene then used their truncheons. The NYPD's own internal report on the riot emphasised that 'extensive broadcasting of film and video taken by the media and private citizens' meant that 'most residents of the city' had witnessed police officers 'striking demonstrators'—and this was 'appalling behaviour', not only in the eyes of the rioters, the news commentators and the private citizens whose video record was broadcast by the television stations citywide, but also in the eyes of senior police officers themselves.[41]

In such circumstances the police, acting on behalf of local residents, businesses and the public, lacked any incentive to attempt to retake public thoroughfares and public places for general use. The public that was not immediately affected by the restrictions on their lives imposed by violence, drug use and the myriad associated public nuisances had been persuaded that drug use was harmless, violence a justified reaction to economic deprivation or racial discrimination, and homelessness always the consequence of society's harshness or indifference.

In Britain as well as the United States influential academic commentators and broadsheet journalists were astonishingly successful in propagating the view—it can still be heard, even today—that crime, violence, and public nuisance had not increased at all. These things had been as prevalent or worse in the past, and the ignorant, hysterical and contemptible general public was simply in the grip of one of its periodic bouts of 'moral panic'.[42] If there was no new problem, then obviously nothing new needed to be done to solve it, least of all by the police.

People who could do so abandoned the invaded areas of the city in droves. In mid-town Manhattan, the great shops and theatres languished. Tourists gave the city a wide berth. Potential investors were deterred from considering New York as a destination for their developments. Whole 'projects' (municipal and federal housing estates) were abandoned to drugs and violence.

In the early- to mid-1980s apocalyptic projections of existing trends continued to draw a picture of drug-fuelled anarchy on the streets, with young criminals running amok with machine guns, in a city being bled dry by the expense of caring for AIDS victims and babies addicted to crack cocaine.[43]

The peaceable control of the real situation that these fantasies reflected, on behalf of the people whose 'lifestyles' did not prevent the pursuit of other life-styles, would have to wait until the culture of 'the victim of society' and 'the rights of the deviant' had shifted in favour of the rights of the law-abiding and the victim of the criminal; and until the NYPD had the sheer numbers to concentrate an overwhelming weight of police officers' bodies in opposition to an unco-operative crowd.

In 1975 there had been 83,000 robberies in New York City—as in England, this was already a vast rise on 1955, when the New York robbery figure had been 7,400. (The figure of 7,400 robberies was thought to be amazingly high by English standards in 1955. It is more likely today that both English and American commentators will deny that it could have ever been so low.) By 1981 there were 107,000 robberies. From 1982, police numbers slowly built up again. But the police culture of rushing in powerful cars to the scene of major crime did not weaken. Robberies were cut to some extent, just as they have been cut with the extraordinary and temporary resources, similar to Britain's ten-city Street Crime Initiative and London's Operation Safer Streets.

In 1991, as assistant commissioner, Ray Kelly was instrumental in securing a tax aimed at increasing the number of NYPD police officers by 7,000 under the Mayor David Dinkins' Safe City/Safe Streets programme. As commissioner in 1992 he targeted quality-of-life street nuisances and street crimes. Street robberies were cut from 100,000 in 1990 to 86,000 in 1993.[44]

In 1994 Rudolph Giuliani was elected mayor of New York City on the promise that he would deal with crime. Plenty of politicians before the 1990s had promised to be tough on crime and the causes of crime, and gained the kudos of being tough (or sustaining the image of being tough), whatever happened to the crime figures themselves. Before 1991, too, there had been much talk of 'citizen/police partnership', 'community policing', 'police problem-solving' and so forth.[45] Mayor Giuliani publicly undertook to *reduce* crime by *applying* these strategies, a very different sort of promise. He appointed as his first police commissioner William Bratton, who was fresh from his triumphs in restoring security to the subway as chief of New York's transport police.

More police officers on the streets

As already noted, Giuliani greatly expanded the size of New York's police force. The 'uniformed headcount' was 28,700 in 1993. By the end of 1994 it was 30,500, and by the year 2000 it was 40,300.[46]

Several functions that in England are performed by the Metropolitan Police, in the United States are performed not by New York's police department, but by the FBI, the CIA or other special agencies. In so far as the sheer number of police officers present on the streets is an element in controlling street crime, this fact simply strengthens the case for more police officers, so that more can be put on the streets to carry out low-level policing (so long as that is what they are actually used for).

Low-level policing

With the larger number of officers at their disposal, Giuliani and Bratton bore down heavily on 'harmless' quality-of-life social nuisances and 'victimless' crimes that nevertheless were the seedbed of those crimes that did have victims, and of dangerous social disorder—prostitutes soliciting on the streets; people committing drug misdemeanours as well as drug felonies on the streets, in the parks and in derelict corners of the city; graffitists; over-boisterous, drunken youths; over-loud users in public of 'foul language'; unauthorised street vendors; squeegee men; aggressive and multitudinous beggars—all the things that had gradually become too trivial for the old beleaguered police to bother about, especially when progressive public opinion insisted that it was quite wrong to bother about them anyway.

The enforcement of the law against minor crimes, non-criminal breaches of the peace and 'quality of life' offences, was achieved by the increased visibility and accessibility of many more officers on foot patrol. 'Enforcement' did not mean rigidity of response. According to the circumstances of the infringement, the police officer's response in policy terms properly ranged from citations and arrests at one extreme to admonitions and reminders at the other.

Getting prostitutes off the streets (much the easiest police job compared with removing drug dealers and drug users or the homeless, whether mentally ill or not) was the start of the virtuous circle, just as allowing the prostitutes to occupy the streets had been the start of the vicious circle. With the disorderly street-life engendered by street prostitution gone, the drug dealers left. With the prostitutes' clients gone, people to rob and cars to steal easily left too, and so the robbers left. The streets were once again occupied by people whose interest was in freedom to go about their own business, considerate of other people's rights to go about their own business. Public places were once again occupied by the endless variety of the well behaved, instead of the bleak and threatening monotony of a city's low life.

Bryant Park was closed for two years. It was re-opened as a place that could be enjoyed by thousands of workers and visitors a day, by being also a place that made it difficult for a few tens or hundreds of drug users, drug dealers and homeless people to occupy it permanently as their own.

The Regents of NYU appealed to the police to free Washington Square Park from prostitutes and drug dealers and users. A permanent NYPD command centre was placed in the park, and without its crack and its guns Washington Square Park became available once more for general use by large numbers of students, residents, workers and tourists.

The NYPD's policy from 1994 was a major attempt to take back from criminals, and sub-criminal perpetrators of petty and (in the short run) 'victimless' offences, or unpleasant users, control of public spaces (and definitions of what is acceptable behaviour in public) and return it to people who are respectful of the rights of others to a socially peaceable and physically salubrious environment. The agent of change was the officer on foot patrol, as the member of the community who is clearly authorised and readily available to *take responsibility* for responding decisively to criminal conduct and sub-criminal neighbourhood disorder and nuisance. In some major city-centres the police officer had been supplemented by privately uniformed 'public safety officers', prior to the institution of the Giuliani/Bratton policing regime. With no more authority than any other citizen, they acted solely by being present on the streets as people who would take responsibility for dealing with any crime or other banned activity, in their case by calling in the NYPD foot patrol officers or further police backup.[47]

Away from the glamour of 42nd Street and Broadway, in Harlem's five police precincts there were 6,500 robberies in 1981.[48] This had been reduced to 4,800 by 1990—a reduction of 26 per cent. But the cuts in the numbers of robberies were much greater in the 1990s under the *steady and consistent pressure* of police commissioner Bratton's policies.[49] Robberies dropped from the 4,800 of 1990, to 1,700 in the year 2000 (a cut of 65 per cent). In the most notorious of New York's precincts, precinct 67 in South Brooklyn, the numbers were cut in the 1990s, to almost exactly the same extent—from 2,200 robberies in 1990 to 743 in the year 2000 (also a cut of 65 per cent). In 1990 there were 2,300 cases of murder and manslaughter in New York. In 2001 there were 642.[50]

For 30 years the police (not only in New York and the United States) had been increasingly defined—and had thus increasingly come to define themselves—as oppressors of working-class communities. But statistical data have increasingly made evident what common sense had always indicated, that the most victimised part of the community looks most anxiously to the police for protection. The latest US Criminal Victimisation Survey indicates that while 54 per cent of white victims of robbery reported the crime to the police, 60 per cent of black victims did so.[51]

These cuts in robberies of 65 per cent in Harlem and South Brooklyn in the 1990s, and a cut in robberies of 67 per cent from 1993 to 2000 in New York citywide, incidentally puts paid to the silly but often repeated idea that the possession of mobile phones 'explains' the rise in robbery in London. There were as many young people flaunting their mobile phones on the streets of Harlem's precincts and precinct 67 when robbery was dramatically falling, as there were in Lambeth, where only recently inroads have been made into a decade's surge in street crime.

More generally, it puts paid to the argument that the reason for the difference between the robbery rates of the England of the interwar period, and England of the 1990s and today, was that before the war 'there was nothing to pinch', with the implication that in those days if there had been any working-class woman about with money in her purse, or any child carrying home the precious groceries, they would have been mugged.

A cousin of one of the authors, handicapped in speech and posture from childhood as a result of contracting poliomyelitis, worked as a teenager as an odd-job boy in the Sunderland Corporation Transport Department. One of his jobs on a Monday was to carry the weekend's tram and bus takings, much of it copper and silver, over to Barclay's bank in the town … on the tram. In the foyer he enjoyed the opportunity to mingle with the friendly young girls from the department stores round about, like Blackett's and Binns—the privileged shop assistants whose perk it was to get out of the shop for a few minutes to walk round to the bank with cloth bags full of Saturday's takings in their hands.

It was long before being robbed or attacked entered his or anybody else's head. On the rare occasions that he was pestered as a 'cripple', the culprits were immediately put in order by passers-by, or other people around on a social occasion, or by the sight of 'a poliss'. Once he simply limped into the Central Fire Station to protect himself from something little worse than banter, and his verbal tormentors fled as the town's burly firemen piled out to deal with them. This is what is now routinely referred to by people who have no experience of it as 'the golden age that never existed'.

Comstat

Giuliani and Bratton imposed a system that made it incumbent upon precinct commanders to justify their leadership at police headquarters by showing results in one thing only—crime reduction. This involved much more than trivial crime. The sinews of the system were the data collected for and analysed and presented by a computer system known as Comstat. Police headquarters knew quickly what was happening in the precincts. Each precinct commander had to be ready to come to police headquarters at short notice to describe and assess his or her tactics, and the results that were being obtained in the precinct. Many old-guard precinct commanders were demoted, and many resigned. Many young officers brought their merits immediately to the attention of the commissioner in face-to-face meetings, and secured rapid promotion. On a daily basis precinct commanders were expected by their superior officers to identify particular outbreaks of robbery or other crimes, and quickly devise tactics to combat them. Woe betide the commander who did not spot a problem in his precinct before his superiors at police headquarters saw it! Woe betide the precinct commander who did not produce effective strategies for dealing with a crime problem in his precinct! Woe betide the precinct commander who did not deliver the one thing that now counted: crime reduction, and especially the reduction of street crime!

Multi-agency work

A third change was 'multi-agency' work. The political and administrative set-up in New York facilitates the effective use of multi-agency approaches to the solution of street-crime problems. Multi-agency work did not mean setting up a talking shop. It meant, for example, that if a dark and derelict part of a neighbourhood was being used for drug dealing and drug use, the sanitation department would be instructed to clear the site of abandoned cars and other rubbish. The transportation department would be instructed to fence the site. The site would be strongly lit with vandal-proof lamps. The drug dealers' and drug users' territory would be permanently taken away from them and permanently reoccupied by the city as a salubrious part of the neighbourhood.

In the case of New York the whole point of the 'multi-agency approach' was to focus responsibility for multi-agency success on the police's objectives in controlling street crime, and within the NYPD to focus accountability on each local police commander.

The British 'partnerships' between the police and usually quite junior officers sent by the local director of education, the director of social services, the probation office and so on are wrapped in the same language as that used in New York. The effects, however (if not the more or less conscious purpose), are that attention is distracted from street crime to easier topics. Not only effective policing, but also (very often mainly) uncontroversial targets are discussed that are only tangentially or in the long term, and possibly but not certainly, one of the means of controlling street crime—notably changes in police staffing proportions. Where street crime remains as a topic, responsibility for combating it by policing methods in the here and now is dissipated.

The professionally inculcated world-view of, for example, social-work partners, is very long-term and speculative. It is that street crime would disappear if the standard of living of the street criminals were to be raised to some at present unknowable extent; or if the gap between the rich and poor were narrower; or if jobs of a certain intrinsic content, wage level, and other working conditions were available; or if the educational system provided at present unspecifiable 'sufficient' resources of an at present unpredictably 'suitable' kind; or if a large enough proportion of the population could be persuaded to change their opinions of what they consider is worthy of 'respect'; or if racism, paternalism, ageism, strong attachments to one's moral code or religious faith and so on were all dissolved in a universal dissensus of tolerant *anomie*.[52]

That Britain should succeed in tackling the problem of street crime by gradually finding and providing the

correct blend of techniques, buildings, trained personnel and financial resources that the electorate or
government would be willing to provide and adopt is,
of course, the hope and aim of all people of good will.
But in the meantime the police have to tackle the
problem of street crime with the resources they have
and with the outside culture that exists; prior to the
discovery and implementation of efficacious and
acceptable reforms, there will be criminals in British
society. It is precisely because elusive and efficacious
reform lies in the future that policing as such has its
effective part to play in the present.

That we are far from discovering the right formula,
even assuming the availability of virtually unlimited
financial resources, and that police officers tread the
wrong path if they follow in the wake of social workers, was sharply confirmed in the recent case of
Richard Wilding. Until he was 13 he was the benefi-
ciary of the not inexpensive best that had been actually made available to him in the social-welfare and
state-education systems. He was then taught individu-
ally for half the school week by a specialist teacher at
home, and for the other half at a unit by staff trained
as expertly as the system knows how, and has been
willing to afford. The cost was £19,000 a year (the
annual school fees at Eton were £13,000 at the time).
As a broadly smiling, apparently happy, sturdy and
confident 20-year-old, he was pictured in January
2003 emerging from the court that had sentenced him
to two years 'community rehabilitation'. He had been
convicted as a burglar, having been caught breaking
into the same house twice in three days. The best
efforts of the existing system had also proven defective
in socialising his own mother. When Richard was
about nine years old, she had punched a housing

officer and pushed him down a flight of stairs when he had visited the family dwelling provided for her by the local council. After extensive hospital treatment, the officer was registered as 80 per cent disabled, and had to retire on medical grounds.[53]

Retaking the city centre and residential areas

The Times Square district, Washington Square Park and Bryant Park provide striking and particularly clear examples of this policy of the permanent reoccupation of neighbourhood territory for pleasant use of the general public, and not just for the use of criminal or nuisance-creating elements in the city's parks and streets.

The task was prolonged by the success of propaganda that assimilated criminals and public nuisances in public places to the unintentionally homeless, and homelessness to a constitutionally protected right to free expression.

In some cases—the heavy-handed aspect of the Giuliani/Bratton policy—to deny criminals a territory from which to operate, the NYPD would close off to any but the residents, and other people authorised by the NYPD, whole blocks of properties identified as being among the most badly affected by drug dealing and drug use. The old police tactics had been to arrest dealers—who were immediately replaced by others in the same locality. But drug dealers permanently deprived of their territory did not find it easy to find another place from which to operate, if for no other reason than that it was difficult to encroach on areas already occupied by rivals. Arrests as the criterion of success were now seen to have been as misleading as body counts of Vietcong as the criterion of success. No real advantage was gained where either aim was accomplished. What had been essential then in the case of war, was essential now in the case of crime and disorder: to take and hold permanently the enemy's territory.

The theory of 'broken-windows' policing

Whether Mayor Giuliani and Police Commissioner Bratton were right or wrong in what they did, they were not cynically picking easy targets. They were acting on the theory that 'one thing leads to another'—the common-sense view that Jane Jacobs put at the centre of her book on the death of great cities, that, civically, if you look after the behavioural pennies, the behavioural pounds will look after themselves.[54] The principal exponent of this theory, called by him 'broken-windows' policing, was George Kelling, and he played a prominent role in the formulation and implementation of the Giuliani/Bratton innovations.

He emphasised that any city can handle with tolerance, compassion or generosity a few rowdy youths, a few scroungers, a few drug users, a few muggers, a few people who sleep in shop doorways or drink cider in the park, a few beggars, or even many tractable derelicts on a city's Skid Row, like New York's Bowery up to the 1970s, with its many Missions and flop houses. At some point, however, the growth of the numbers of those who are intractable adversely affects the whole functioning of the city. Public thoroughfares and parks, and semi-public facilities like railway carriages, fall under their control. A vicious circle sets in as caution or distaste keeps other people off the streets. In its small beginnings, the risk may be slight that the beggar or gang of youths in the underpass will turn unpleasant or criminally violent. But if such a new threat to dignity or safety does appear, many a 70-year-old who formerly used the underpass will apply the precautionary principle, the principle of avoiding a small risk of great damage, and be deterred from visiting the town. The unfrequented underpass then becomes an increasingly unsightly and rubbish-strewn playground of boisterous youths and a market for illicit drugs, deterring still more members of the general public from using it. The disorderly milieu attracts more disorderliness into the streets and local public houses. As the homes and shops round about are broken into and cars defaced or stolen, the neigh-bourhood deteriorates further. If the police, much more if the public try to intervene now, there is an increased likelihood that they will be attacked by an unruly mob protecting their own.[55] This catalytic role of unchecked 'trivial' and 'victimless' crimes was emphasised in NYPD's policing after 1993.[56]

Kelling and Sousa tested the four most frequently adduced arguments for the decline in crime by the statistical analysis of trends in crime and social conditions in different New York police precincts. The results showed that neither the improvement in the economy (the decline in the rate of unemployment), nor the decline in the use of crack cocaine, nor the reduction in the number of young males, was signifi-cantly associated with the decline in the crime rate in the different precincts.

The change significantly associated with crime reduction statistically was the changed activity of the reformed New York police.[57]

'Broken-windows' policing elsewhere in America and England

John Timoney, from his experience as deputy commis-sioner in the NYPD, took 'broken-windows' policing,

Comstat, the frequent meetings with precinct commanders, and the other features of the Giuliani regime to Philadelphia, and enjoyed the same sort of success in bringing down the crime figures.

One of his main targets was Kensington, a crime-ridden black neighbourhood of Philadelphia. He attacked the 'petty' as well as the 'serious' drug users and dealers who had been increasingly ignored by a demoralised police force that, with the approval of main-stream media, had come to rationalise its self-defined impotence as toleration of what was ethnically 'cultural'.

Police Commissioner Timoney's chief of staff was formerly a Home Office official. In Britain, he said, most police officers still did not think they could do anything about stopping crime going up, much less do anything about bringing crime down. 'No one is blamed when crime goes up, unemployment and race are blamed instead.'[58]

In England, something very close to 'broken windows' was pragmatically developed in Hartlepool, independently, by Ray Mallon (whose successful policing was so popular with the general public that in 2002 he was elected American-type executive mayor of Middlesbrough on a landslide vote). He, too, showed that while deep social changes meant that the police could not cut crime figures back to the levels of even the 1970s, by their efforts they could cut existing levels by at least 30 per cent.

He successfully attacked the debilitating belief that the police, like much of the rest of the population, had absorbed over the course of 30 or 40 years: that crime was caused by poverty, homelessness, exclusion from educational opportunities, unemployment and so forth. On this view, next to nothing could be done about crime by the police except to react to offences when they occurred, and just about everything could be done about it by politicians if only they showed enough compassion.

He was, in effect, his own precinct commander, and on the small scale of Hartlepool was able to obtain New-York-scale cuts in crime without an increase in police numbers, simply by greatly raising the morale of force at his disposal, and generating almost universal good will in areas afflicted by crime, drugs and anti-social nuisances. An important element in his success was that he took it upon himself to 'define the situation' to the public and the media, and not leave it to 'expert' comment from academics and tendentious comment from the advocates of every 'victim' but the criminal's.[59]

The eventual recognition of the scale of the crime problem was belated in England as compared with the United States. One of the reasons for this was the much stronger insulation of the criminal justice system in England from popular opinion. Another was the strength and persistence of the doctrine in the universities, and therefore among influential journalists, senior politicians and bureaucrats, that the growth in crime was not really happening—it was an illusion created by the perennial moral panic of 'respectable' people and the ignorant hysteria of the redtop press.[60]

In 2001/02, 74 per cent of adults in England and Wales still thought that the police did at least a fairly good job. But 20 years before, 92 per cent of adults had thought that. Between 1982 and 1992 the percentage of those thinking the police did a very good job roughly halved from 43 per cent to 24 per cent. It roughly halved again between 1992 and 2002, from 24 per cent to only 14 per cent.[61]

In May 2001 the Home Office required every police force in England and Wales to report on measures they had taken to ensure that police were visible in every ward. Visibility programmes typically meant that one or two officers were allocated foot-patrol duties as an aspect of their designation as 'community beat managers'. For a ward of 20,000, for example, the sole community beat manager might be required to be on foot patrol for 20 of the week's 168 hours. The explicit emphasis was on the 'reassurance' of members of the general public, not on the actual prevention of crime or disorder. Visibility was therefore sometimes, though not by any means always, treated as a grudging concession that had to be accorded to the benighted public, who were foolish enough to think that their fears were justified and that watch and ward policing worked.

But the pressure of public opinion on politicians and the police did lead to some valuable innovations. For example, in a ward in Sunderland with high crime rates and a street-drug problem controlled by mafia-like local families, the police stationed five or six officers, including two or three 'community beat officers', in the area's primary school. The original idea was simply to find local accommodation for the 'broken-windows'-type team.

The results of this operation were so favourable that the scheme attracted interest from television producers from France and Australia, as well as from our own national networks. *Le Parisien*, the local newspaper of the crime-ridden district of Seine-Saint-Denis, featured the scheme under the headline: 'The war on crime and disorder: solutions that work'. 'The methods were radical. The results were spectacular.'[62]

The head of the school reported that, when the police initially appeared, their first view was of a large

new hostile scrawl on the school wall: 'Big Brother!'
The officers were greeted by some of the pupils, 3 to 11
year olds, with verbal insults and raised fingers. But
in the space of two years, under the régime of 'broken-
windows' policing, crime in the ward as a whole fell by
a third. In the school incidents of violence fell by 95
per cent.

What was of particular interest were the side effects
on the school's young pupils of daily seeing 'broken-
windows' police officers at close quarters. The police
officers did not keep order in the school, but in the
local community.[63] The head said that in an area in
which 80 per cent of the parents were wholly depend-
ent on state benefits, for many of the pupils the police
officer in the school, engaged in 'broken-windows'
police work, provided them with their only model of
what it was to exercise steady and benign authority
without the use of violence as a man and a parent. In
her opinion, it was essential that her pupils should
experience all this before the age of 11. Children
whose language was peppered with swear words, and
whose attitude was to be violent towards others, were
offered new reference points when they were able see
the secure and tranquil benefits of law and order being
restored in their school and improved in their streets
by people they knew and trusted. By the time the
children were ready for Youth Justice Teams and the
like (and even more, by the time they had to be dealt
with by the prisons), it was too late for many of them.
They would have adopted violence, drug taking and
delinquency too firmly as a way of handling their lives.

In 1991 Princess Anne visited the school to honour
the project; by June 2002 the Prime Minister, Tony
Blair, 'notably inspired' (as *Le Parisien* put it), had
been instrumental in extending something like the
scheme to about sixty other schools; and in January

2003 it was the subject of a major conference addressed by the Minister for Schools, David Milliband.[64]

More or less properly understood, and more or less actually applied, aspects of all or some of the New York model of 'broken-windows' policing appeared in many other places in the United States, and some other places in England.

New York City in 2003

The NYPD, helped by the Business Improvement District (BID) 'public safety police' again keeps the peace in Times Square.[65] The Port Authority Bus Terminal is busy, clean and pleasant.

By early 2003, late in the evening, if you asked the way in some formerly notorious neighbourhoods, you would be given the walking directions for several blocks, without any warning or premonition of danger. The new-found safety of New York's streets was an element in its being selected as the American city that should bid to host the Olympic Games.

New Yorkers now talk of the time when Bryant Park and other public spaces were unusable by ordinary people because they were occupied by cannabis and heroin dealers and users; when a wide area on Eighth Avenue at the Port Authority terminal was avoided for the same reason; and when the threat of being robbed was pervasive, as old, forgotten, far-off things and battles long ago. In such localities today only the occasional beggar is to be seen, like the man in Times Square whose placard cheerfully asks for money for drink and drugs, accompanied by the claim that he deserves to be rewarded for his honesty.

Given the great increase in the numbers of police officers, Mayor Giuliani's campaigns of low-level policing by foot patrols, Comstat-driven control of precinct commanders, together with multi-agency problem-solving partnerships (not multi-agency talking shops) and the robust reoccupation of the streets and residential areas by the forces of law and order, were so successful in combating higher-level crimes like robbery, that in his second term he faced the revival of the elite criticism that had been hegemonic from the mid-1960s to the late 1980s, that disorderly or nuisance elements in New York were being denied the scope for self-expression to which they were entitled by the narrow-minded and uncompassionate respectable majority.[66]

The attack on the World Trade Center (very close to City Hall and police headquarters) had the effect of placing Metropolitan-Police-type burdens on the NYPD—guarding bridges, embassies, railway stations and key tourist areas against terrorists. One thousand officers were assigned to anti-terrorism duties.[67] Renewed financial stringency generally—combined with the short memory some people had, who thought that because New York was markedly freer from street crime now than in the recent past, the police could go on short commons—led to cuts in the police budget. Under the budget for 2003/04, the number of police officers in the NYPD would drop to 37,000 by the summer of 2003.[68]

On the national level, President Clinton's administration had backed 'broken-windows' policing by inaugurating an $8 billion programme to recruit 100,000 locality police officers, the so-called Community Oriented Policing Service (COPS)—a policy that coincided with annual reductions in the crime rate. The Bush administration cut the COPS programme by 80 per cent—coinciding with a two per cent increase in the crime rate.[69]

Kelling attributes the successes of the NYPD in cutting street crime so early and so dramatically—as compared with persistent growth of street crime in England and Wales more or less to the present day—to the NYPD's return to the principles of law enforcement enunciated by Sir Robert Peel as the basis of effective policing, that 'the basic mission for which the police exist is to prevent crime and disorder' by watch and ward, and that the proper test of police efficiency is 'the absence of crime and disorder, not the visible evidence of police dealing with them'. And the NYPD was able to return to those principles not only because it obtained the number of 'constables' that enabled it do so, but also because it changed its own culture and, sufficiently, society's culture—the view that the media and the general public took of what the problem was, and what policing could do to combat it.[70]

Perhaps it needed a perceptive American to point all this out to us; and for the England that has neglected them, perhaps it is time to relearn the lessons of low-level policing that she taught to world, from the America that is successfully applying them.

Conclusion

Where the laws of a state or the rules of an organisation are the product of open discussion and representative government free from corruption, freedom of choice to himself and all others is afforded by the conduct of 'the law-abiding citizen' and the 'rule-respecting participant'. By contrast, within the framework of democratically arrived-at rules, other people's freedom is subjected to arbitrary restriction by those who break the law or ignore the rules.

Blue-collar criminals and nuisances, generally petty, as well as often major and ignored white-collar criminals, consider that breaking the rules is beneficial or at least satisfying to themselves. Political fanatics and religious fundamentalists break the rules in their self-righteous belief that this is required by what is socially just or religiously virtuous.

The immediate effects of their offensive behaviour, crimes and outrages are pernicious enough. But more pernicious still (if the individual is not to resort to private violence to uphold community values or, very much worse, succumb to selfish or fanatical lawlessness) is the erosion of liberty that their conduct brings in its train. 'The law-abiding citizen', if he is to defend himself within the law, has to give up some of the freedom he has enjoyed in a society of other considerate and law-abiding citizens, in order to improve his security against both the petty violators of his liberty and those whose ambition, all in a good cause, is his indiscriminate murder. Law-breakers begin by robbing the law-abiding citizen of his tranquillity, property and bodily safety. They end by robbing him and his children of the benefits of a free society.

Notes

1 Home Office, *Criminal Statistics England and Wales 1991*, Cm 2134, London: TSO, February 1992. The figures on robberies include assaults with attempt to rob.

2 http://www.met.police.uk/crimestatistics/index.htm

3 http://www.nyc.gov/html/nypd/html/auxiliary.html Management Analysis and Planning, Crime Analysis Unit, *Statistical Report: complaints and arrests*, New York: NYPD, different dates of issue.

4 The Policy Exchange, *Going Local: who should run Britain's police?*, London: The Policy Exchange, January 2003.

5 Home Office press release 272/2002, 14 October 2002.

6 See the Metropolitan Police's web site, http://www.met. police.uk/crimestatistics/index.htm

7 Povey, D., Ellis, C. and Nicholas, S., *Crime in England and Wales: quarterly update 12 months to September 2002*, HOSB 02/03, London: Home Office, January 2003, p. 9. Both the wording of the questions and the presentation of the results is highly tendentious. The category of response 'very or fairly' confident tells us only that all the respondents in that category were at least 'fairly' confident, and no more. The question about the treatment of those accused of committing a crime—which includes many who did commit a crime—asks quite properly about how well the system 'respects' their 'rights'. But the same question logically applies with equal and full force to the victims of crime—how far does the system protect their rights, especially the crucial right so far as the criminal justice system is concerned— its raison d'être—the right to pursue their lawful business, protected from law-breakers and nuisances? But the question refers not to victims' rights but to the victims' 'needs'. Only 23 per cent had any confidence that the system was effective in dealing with young people accused of crime, a response to a question that comes

nearer to the citizens' right to protection from criminals than the wishy-washy 'needs' question.

8 Management Analysis and Planning, Crime Analysis Unit, *Statistical Report: complaints and arrests*.

9 They will be comparable when the system settles down.

10 Simmons, J. and colleagues, *Crime in England and Wales 2001/2002*, HOSB 07/02, London: Home Office, July 2002.

11 In a longer perspective still, the historical amnesia that leads to a concentration on the figures of the last ten or twenty years is even more misleading. The average annual figure of crimes before the Great War was only 98 *thousand*. In 1955, the number was still less than half a million. Since before the Great War, the population has not even doubled. The crime rate has multiplied 44 times and more. Whatever might be demonstrated and not just asserted about defects in the numbers, the relentless *rise*, slow until about 1955, rapid since 1955, falling since 1992, cannot be explained away as a statistical artefact. *Criminal Statistics England and Wales*, London: HMSO, then TSO, annually since 1857.

12 Povey, Ellis and Nicholas, *Crime in England and Wales: quarterly update 12 months to September 2002*, January 2003, p. 1. Emphasis added.

13 The 1972 figures are to be found in Home Office, *Criminal Statistics England and Wales 1978*, Cmnd. 7670, London, HMSO, 1979.

14 The current figures are to be found in Flood-Page, C. and Taylor, J. (eds.), *Crime in England and Wales 2001/2002: supplementary volume*, HORB 01/03, London: Home Office, January 2003, and Povey, Ellis and Nicholas, *Crime in England and Wales: quarterly update 12 months to September 2002*, January 2003.

15 http://www.met.police.uk/crimestatistics/index.htm

16 'Electronic eyes turn seedy flats into desirable residences', *Guardian*, 6 January 1999.

17 Welsh, B.C. and Farrington, D.P., *Crime Prevention Effects of Closed Circuit Television: a systematic review*, HORS No. 252, London: Home Office, August 2002.

18 *Daily Telegraph*, 12 September 2002.

19 For the purposes of the Home Office's Street Crimes Initiative, 'street crime' comprises robbery, snatch theft, the illegal use and possession of firearms and carjacking. Within the terms of reference of the Street Crime Initiative, carjacking is defined as the theft of a vehicle in use, using violence or the threat of violence. (Direct communication with the Home Office.) In practice, the Home Office Street Crime Initiative, at any rate up to September 2002, used simply robbery—not robbery only of personal property, and not robbery of a vehicle in use, and not the illegal use or possession of firearms—sometimes with and sometimes without the figures for snatch theft. Carjacking offences were published in *Crime in England and Wales 2001/2002*, HOSB 07/02 as *part of* the robbery figures, since carjacking is theft involving violence.

20 The effect of the National Crime Recording Standard (NCRS) is to inflate the recorded crime numbers as compared with those recorded on the old basis by 10 per cent. In the case of the figures for violence against the person the NCRS causes an inflation of the numbers by 23 per cent. But the figures for robbery are inflated by only three per cent. (Povey and colleagues, 2003, p. 5.)

The possibility of using different dates for the purposes of comparison, and the inclusion of several offences within the term 'street crime', or alternatively the studied vagueness of what offences are included, has the advantage of enabling those whose presentation can be expected to be published and broadcast ostentatiously to include those figures that are favourable to their propaganda purpose, and exclude surreptitiously those that are unfavourable to it. The Home Office's news release of 12 September 2002 chose to compare the March 2002 figure with the August 2002 figure, a rare procedure among statisticians, who almost invariably

compare a month's figures with the same month in
previous years.

21 Simmons and colleagues, *Crime in England and Wales
    2001/2002*, 2002.

22 Metropolitan Police Service, *Annual Report 2000/01*,
    London: Metropolitan Police Authority and Metropolitan
    Police, 2002, p. 9.

23 *Criminal Statistics England and Wales* for the year 1931
    points to the 'problem' of the increase in robberies since
    the early 1920s. The number of robberies known to the
    police 'averaged 177 in the years 1920-24. By 1927 the
    number had declined to 110. Since 1927 there has been
    an increase'. The 'problem' was an increase in the Metro-
    politan Police area to 104, and in the rest of England and
    Wales to the same figure, making a total figure of 208
    robberies for the whole *year* in the whole of the *country*.
    Home Office, *Criminal Statistics England and Wales
    1931*, Cmd. 4360, London: HMSO, May 1933. Thus, *after*
    the Metropolitan Police had thrown extra and temporary
    resources at the problem in Operation Safe Streets, there
    were still more than twice the number of robberies of
    personal property in a single month, July 2002, in a
    single London borough, Lambeth, than there had been
    robberies of all types of property in the whole of the
    country in whole of 1927. I quote these statistics recog-
    nising fully that they will not be believed. But having no
    alternative figures, anyone contradicting them has to
    produce some evidence that they were grossly inaccurate
    —by reference, say, to contemporary comment in the
    1920s or 1930s on the lawlessness of British streets. In
    fact contemporary comment uniformly presents a picture
    that is consistent with these figures, and it is impossible
    to conceive that a figure of 208 would have been placidly
    accepted if the situation had been that people knew,
    from their own experience, that robberies were a
    commonplace in their towns or neighbourhoods.

24 Simmons and colleagues, *Crime in England and Wales
    2001/2002*, 2002.

25 'Paddick: my story', *Daily Mirror*, 25 March 2002.

26 New York City Police Department, *Annual Reports 1870-*, New York: City of New York, annually from 1870, no copies traced after 1988. The police numbers are 'police officers enrolled'.

27 Civilian Complaint Review Board (CCRB), *Annual Status Report 2000*, New York: CCRB, 2001; and http://www.nyc.gov./html/ccrb/home.html
     The ratios are calculated on the unrounded figures, and do not always exactly correspond to the rounded figures shown in the text.

28 *Criminal Statistics England and Wales 1993: supplementary tables*, Vol. 3, London: Government Statistical Service, November 1994. *Metropolitan Police Fund Estimates 1992/93*, Cm 2039, London: TSO, September 1992.

29 Smith, C., Rundle, S. and Hosking, R., *Police Service Strength England and Wales, 31 March 2002*, 10/02, London: TSO, September 2002.

30 Metropolitan Police monthly statistics: http://www.met.police.uk/crime statistics/ index.htm

31 The table's crime statistics are from *Criminal Statistics England and Wales*, London: HMSO, annually. The police numbers 1971 to 2001 are taken from: http://www.statistics.gov.uk/STATBASE/Expodata/Spreadsheets/D3574.xls. Looking further back, to the interwar period, the number of police officers in England and Wales had roughly doubled (129,000 in 2002 as compared with 59,000 in 1931). But the 129,000 officers in 2002 had to deal with 31 times the number of reported crimes (at least 5 million in 2002 as compared with 159,000 in 1931). In 1921 there were 57,000 officers to deal with only 103,000 reported crimes—only 2 reported crimes per officer per year, as contrasted with the 44 in 2001. The figure for 2001/02, 129,600 police officers, is given in Smith, Rundle and Hosking, *Police Service Strength*, 2002. The 1921 and 1931 police numbers are given in

President of the Board of Trade, *Statistical Abstract of the United Kingdom*, No. 76, Cmd. 4233, London: HMSO, 1933.

32 Londoners might not be as familiar as are provincials with the daily news of small nuisances in their neighbourhoods that the victims of the nuisances feel are properly a matter of the immediate presence of a police officer in the here and now, but that are treated by the police as somebody else's problem, that will be solved at some time in the indefinite future by means as yet, to say the least, of undemonstrated efficacy. Such stories are a staple of the provinces' evening news media. The following accounts appear in a single edition of the *Sunderland Echo*:

> A group of neighbours claim that they have suffered for two years from 'trouble makers' who race cars past their houses, burn rubbish and furniture in the street, vandalise property, and threaten and abuse them. People are afraid to leave their homes, and children are not allowed out to play. One woman says that the trouble makers have threatened to kill her three children, two of whom are handicapped. They say that the police have done nothing. A police sergeant is quoted as saying, 'We are working closely with the residents' association and the council to find some solutions. There are discussions taking place regarding better facilities for young people and traffic calming measures but of course these things take time'.

Another report dealt with a meeting place near a stream-side path for drinking and drug taking. The beer cans, the squalor and the possible presence of the people taking drugs effectively closed off the path to all other users and all other uses. Whatever the personal and *social* reasons for the young people being there and doing that, and however important it was to find a solution to the underlying causes, the presence of a constable was the solution to their monopolising, for the narrow purposes of their own small group, a facility that would otherwise be used by many people for many purposes. A spokesman said that the Council had 'initiated a review of young people's provision in the city' that would 'focus on meeting the future play demands for informal play provision'.

A third report says that about 40 people concerned about another street had united to demand help from the police. The people who have consideration for the freedom of other people to pursue their varied activities, the 'decent' people, had to live with 'terrible problems' of drink and drugs, all-night parties, damage to their property and fires in the street. The final straw came when a 70-year-old woman was mugged and given two black eyes. The problem was transferred partly to the residents. They were the people the police needed to control, for they were threatening to deal with the disorderly elements themselves. ('Defiant villagers' message to the police: DEAL WITH THE YOBS OR WE WILL!') Partly it was transferred to private landlordism and the state of the dwellings. 'We do not condone people to turn vigilante ... In the long term, the Community Safety Partnership is working on a private landlord scheme to help improve stock.' *Sunderland Echo*, 12 September 2002.

There is a large fund of good will towards the police. In public opinion polls they always rank much higher than any group that contains even their law-abiding critics, such as lawyers, politicians and journalists (not to mention how much higher they rank than their critics among ordinary law-breakers and those who, from whatever high-minded or pecuniary motive, take the law-breakers' side). At any rate in smaller provincial cities the police have never been 'the filth' as they are, for example, to that portion of London's East End that flocked to a Kray funeral to pay homage to the memory of a notorious gangster. They have never been 'pigs', as they are to students following an American fashion set by drug users in the 1960s. In the towns and smaller cities of England, they have never had a worse generally-used label than the one they have now, 'the chocolate fireguards'. They are called the chocolate fireguards not to blame them, but to express the reality of the results of enormous disproportion between, on the one hand, the small growth in the number of police officers and, on the other, the large growth in incidents of crime, disorder and nuisance.

33 Mark, Sir Robert, *In the Office of Constable: an autobiography*, London: Collins, 1978.

34 Magnet, M., *The Dream and the Nightmare: the sixties' legacy to the underclass*, New York: Morrow, 1993.

35 New York's 'fiscal crisis' began in 1975 during the mayoralty of A.D. Beame, and continued during the first years of the mayoralty of Edward Koch. The city did not recover until 1983, when Koch's administration managed a successful issuance of new city notes.

36 New York City Police Department, *Annual Report 1968*, New York: City of New York, 1969.

37 New York City Police Department, *Annual Report 1974*, New York: City of New York, 1975.

38 New York City Police Department, *Annual Report 1982*, New York: City of New York, 1983.

39 Epstein, J., *The Great Conspiracy Trial: an essay on law, liberty and the constitution*, New York: Random House, 1970. The classic account of the 1968 riots is Norman Mailer's *Miami and the Siege of Chicago: an informal history of the American political conventions of 1968*, Harmondsworth: Penguin, 1969.

40 Dennis, N., Erdos, G. and Al-Shahi, A., *Racist Murder and Pressure Group Politics: the Macpherson report and the police*, London: Civitas, 2000.

41 *Report of Chief of Department to the Police Commissioner on the Tompkins Square Park Incident*, New York: NYPD, 23 August 1988.

42 Dennis, N., *Rising Crime and the Dismembered Family: how conformist intellectuals have campaigned against common sense*, London: Civitas, 1993.

43 Burns, R. and Saunders, J., *New York: an illustrated history*, New York: Knopf, 1999.

44 Management Analysis and Planning, Crime Analysis Unit, *Statistical Report: complaints and arrests*, New York: NYPD, different dates of issue.

45 See, for example, *Policing New York City in the 1990s: the strategy for community policing*, New York: NYPD, January 1991; *Problem Solving Annual for Community Police Officers: disorderly groups*, New York: NYPD, October 1993.

46 New York City Civilian Review Board, *Status Report 2000*, New York: CCRB, 2001, graph 2, entitled 'NYPD average uniformed headcount'. My thanks are due to William H. Sousa, of the Police Institute, School of Criminal Justice, Rutgers University, for this information. The New York City Department of Personnel's *Annual Reports* (New York: City Hall) are intermittent, and give a somewhat different set of statistics. The numbers are complicated by the fact that formerly independent forces were amalgamated with the NYPD during the 1990s, notably the federal Housing Police and the Transport Police. Some 4,000 officers were added to the numbers of NYPD as the Housing Bureau and the Transit Bureau, without adding to the numbers of 'police' in the city.

47 The 'public protection police officers' in Times Square and the surrounding area are the employees of the Times Square Business Improvement District (BID) Inc. This is a not-for-profit organisation set up in 1992 to combat the economically disastrous decline in the area due to it having been invaded and occupied by the heterogeneous 'homeless'. In 2002 it had a $7 million annual budget, $6 million of which is raised by mandatory assessments on local property owners, and $1 million from grants and sponsorships. Besides its security patrols, it undertakes public improvements, for example, in lighting the area, and provides tourist and sanitation services. The power of the propaganda that claimed that all the area's

problems were those of 'homelessness' is echoed in its programme of 'homeless outreach'.

48 Precincts 25, 26, 28, 30 and 32 of Manhattan North Patrol Borough.

49 Bratton, W.J., 'Crime is down in New York City: blame the police', in Dennis, N. (ed.), *Zero Tolerance: policing a free society*, London: Civitas, 1997.

50 Management Analysis and Planning, Crime Analysis Unit, *Statistical Report: complaints and arrests*, New York: NYPD, different dates of issue.

51 Bureau of Justice Statistics, *Criminal Victimization in the United States, 1995: a National Crime Victimization Survey Report*, Washington DC: US Department of Justice, May 2000.

52 *Anomie* is Durkheim's term for a pathological state of social affairs in which culture—shared views about what is true and what is good in this world and the next—does not exist. Durkheim, E., *The Division of Labour in Society* (1893), London: Macmillan, 1933. In its more or less extreme contemporary social-work form *anomie* is highly valued. Every person deems himself or herself, or ought to deem himself or herself, as being wise and good in his or her own eyes. Each person does and must deem all others as equally wise and good in their own eyes. In terms of both what is 'true' and what is 'moral' there is neither any externally accredited 'better' to be aspired to, nor any 'worse' to be shunned. Everything is equally true and good; it is purely a matter of the individual's 'perspective'. Paradoxically, within this system of thought, one judgement remains universal and valid, namely, that it is heinous to adhere firmly to any 'majority' culture. 'Multicultural' societies exist, but in relation to contemporary Western societies the term multiculturalism is often used as a euphemism for *anomie*.

53 *Daily Mail*, 7 January 2003.

54 Jacobs, J., *The Death and Life of Great American Cities*, London: Jonathan Cape, 1962.

55 Kelling, G.L. and Coles, C.M., *Fixing Broken Windows: restoring order and reducing crime in our communities* (1996), New York: Simon and Schuster Touchstone, 1997. Kelling, G.L., 'Toward new images of policing: Herman Goldstein's "problem-oriented" policing', *Law and Social Inquiry*, 17, 3, Summer 1992. Pate, A., Ferrara, A. and Kelling, G.L., 'Foot patrol: a discussion of the issues', in *The Newark Foot Patrol Experiment*, Washington, DC: The Police Foundation, 1981. Kelling, G.L. and others, *The Kansas City Preventive Patrol Experiment*, Washington, DC: The Police Foundation, 1974.

56 See, for example, *Breaking the Cycle of Domestic Violence*, Police Strategy No. 4, New York: NYPD, April 1994; *Reducing Auto-Related Crime in New York,* Police Strategy No. 6, New York: NYPD, February 1995; *Reclaiming the Roads of New York*, Police Strategy No. 8, New York: NYPD, November 1995. One of the earliest successes of the Giuliani/Bratton regime was due to the implementation of the recommendations contained in Kelling, G.L., Julian, M. and Miller, S., *Managing 'Squeegeeing': a problem-solving exercise*, New York: NYPD, 1994. Possibly this report was the first to use the term 'no tolerance'—soon to become 'zero tolerance'. The report said that the problem of 'squeegeeing' could be managed and largely stopped *by patrol officers* if a no tolerance approach was adopted—and it was.

57 Kelling, G.L. and Sousa, W.H. Jr., *Do Police Matter?: an analysis of the impact of New York City's police reforms*, Civic Report No. 22, New York: Center for Civic Innovation, Manhattan Institute, December 2001.

58 Phillips, M., *America's Social Revolution*, London: Civitas and *The Sunday Times*, 2001, p. 37.

59 Dennis, N. (ed.), *Zero Tolerance: policing a free society*, London: Civitas, 1997.

60 Dennis, *Rising Crime and the Dismembered Family*, 1993.

61 Flood-Page, C. and Taylor, J., *Crime in England and Wales: Supplementary Tables*, HOSB 01/03, London: Home Office, January 2003, p. 108. Only 26 per cent thought that other people had respect for the police, though three times that number said they personally had respect for the police.

62 *Le Parisien*, 4 June 2002.

63 The officers did do some direct teaching in class but—an essential point—as familiar friends, not as 'parachuted-in' visitors.

64 *Le Parisien*, 4 June 2002; *Ford and Pallion Community Safety Newsletter*, Sunderland: City of Sunderland Partnership, September 2002; Cops, Kids and Schools, Conference held at the Stadium of Light, Sunderland, 31 January 2003.

65 The BID public safety officers are uniformed, but have no more powers than any other citizen. Most of their time is spent in being helpful to visitors. In case of trouble, their job is to call the police. But because they are on the spot, and *will* call the police, crime and disorder have been reduced to a low level, to the benefit of the vast majority of businesses and people working in and visiting the area.

66 McArdle, A. and Erzen, T. (eds), *Zero Tolerance: quality of life and the new police brutality in New York City*, New York: New York University Press, 2001.

67 As a result, there was a revival of confidence among critics who felt they were once more on familiar territory in condemning the police as the repressive agents of the state. See, for example, Lee, C., 'Nation's largest law enforcement agency vies for total spying power', *The Village Voice*, 18 December 2002.

68 Interview with Ray Kelly, who became police
    commissioner for the second time in 2002. 'New York's
    Top Cop: beat officer at heart', *Christian Science
    Monitor*, 7 January 2003.

69 *Uniform Crime Report*, Washington, DC: FBI, June
    2002. 'Leaked FBI report shows US crime figure on rise
    again', *Daily Telegraph*, 24 June 2002. 'FBI Report:
    major crimes rose 2 per cent in 2001 after 9-year drop',
    USA Today, 24 June 2002.

70 Kelling and Sousa, *Do Police Matter?: an analysis of the
    impact of New York City's police reforms*, 2001.

Independence: The Institute for the Study of Civil Society (CIVITAS) is a registered educational charity (No. 1085494) and a company limited by guarantee (No. 04023541). CIVITAS is financed from a variety of private sources to avoid over-reliance on any single or small group of donors.

All publications are independently refereed. All the Institute's publications seek to further its objective of promoting the advancement of learning. The views expressed are those of the authors, not of the Institute.